DATE DUE

AUG 1 1 2006			
APR 17 '13			
JUL 23 '14			
AUG 10 '15			

© Aladdin Books Ltd 2001

Designed and produced by
Aladdin Books Ltd
28 Percy Street
London W1P 0LD

First published in
the United States in 2001 by
Copper Beech Books,
an imprint of
The Millbrook Press
2 Old New Milford Road
Brookfield, Connecticut 06804

ISBN 0-7613-2167-5

Cataloging-in-Publication data is on
file at the Library of Congress

Printed in Belgium
All rights reserved

Coordinator
Jim Pipe

Design
Flick, Book Design and Graphics

Picture Research
Brian Hunter Smart

My World

At the
Park

by Dr. Alvin Granowsky

Copper Beech Books
Brookfield, Connecticut

2

We love the park.

A day at the park
is a day full of fun.

dogs

Our dog Sammy loves the park.

Sammy can run and play
with the other dogs.

Sammy is so happy at the park.

And when Sammy is happy,
we are happy too.

That is why we love the park.

play on the grass

Dad says, "Go run and play."

The grass is soft.
If we fall down, we don't get hurt.

Dad takes us to a bench to rest.

He says, "When you are happy,
I am happy too."

That is why Dad loves the park.

bench

A woman sits on a bench.

She has a bag full of bread
to feed the pigeons.

pigeons

She tells us that she can
feed the pigeons every day.

That is why she loves the park.

feeding pigeons

Sometimes the woman
gives us some bread.

Then we feed the pigeons.

We feed the squirrel too. It grabs the bread and runs up a tree.

squirrel

That is so much fun to see.

The park has many open spaces.

On cold days we walk in the sun. It helps us stay warm.

In the park there is a lake.

We run down to the edge.

"Don't fall in the water!"
says Dad.

lake

Near the lake there is
a family of ducks.

We can see a mother duck
and five little ducklings.

duck family

Sometimes the ducks say,
"Quack, quack, quack!" to us.

We say, "Quack, quack" to them.

playground

In the park there is a playground.

When we see it, we start to run.
We can't wait to play there.

In the playground
there is a seesaw.

And there are lots of
boys and girls to
play with.

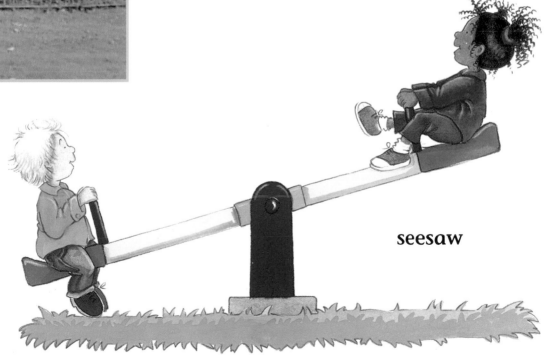

seesaw

The sun is going down.

We know it's time to go,
but we don't want to leave.

We love the park
and never want to leave.

"Don't worry," Dad says.
"We will come back soon."

Here are some words and phrases from the book.

ducks

dogs running

sit on the bench

play on the seesaw

feed the pigeons

squirrel

play with the dog

walk home

Can you use these words to write your own story?